D0887530

TO: Judy

Thanks for the love

Rocky

"800 Sayings by Old Folks
Who Raised Us"

"800 Sayings by Old Folks Who Raised Us"

Wm. Rocky Brown, 3rd

Copyright © 2016 by Wm. Rocky Brown, 3rd.

Library of Congress Control Number: 2016904618
ISBN: Hardcover   978-1-5144-7731-1
                 Softcover   978-1-5144-7730-4
                 eBook   978-1-5144-7729-8

All rights reserved. No part of this book may be reproduced or transmitted in any form or by any means, electronic or mechanical, including photocopying, recording, or by any information storage and retrieval system, without permission in writing from the copyright owner.

Any people depicted in stock imagery provided by Thinkstock are models, and such images are being used for illustrative purposes only.
Certain stock imagery © Thinkstock.

Print information available on the last page.

Rev. date: 03/22/2016

To order additional copies of this book, contact:
Xlibris
1-888-795-4274
www.Xlibris.com
Orders@Xlibris.com
738757

It's is my hope that they will bring you fond memories and laughter and you will share them with your children and grandchildren.

This book is dedicated to my mother Gwendolyn Regina Carraway Brown and my grandmothers: Ethel-Mae Knight Brown (Mother-dear), Halease Moore Wooten-Reid and my great-grandmothers Willie-Mae Knight and Carrie Skipper. My grand's are the women on the cover and that's me at 2 months old. (By the way, that's a design on the chair and not a ribbon in my hair. lol)

Special thanks to my friend Ellen Graham, my Bethany Baptist Church members, my Facebook friends and the contributions I found that were posted on the internet by others who also enjoy these sayings.

Enjoy my friends!
WRB, 3rd

PREFACE

Let me begin by saying that God is the Head of my life, Jesus is my Savior and the Holy Spirit is my Comforter.

Our parents or grandparents, who had roots in the South, raised many of us. Now, along with that Southern raising came the ability to take every day activities or things of nature and turn them into wise sayings. My mother was from Greenville, North Carolina and my grandmother who raised me was from Mobile, Alabama. They both had old sayings from 'Down Home' that took me a while to really understand what they were saying. After talking to others, I realized that I wasn't the only one who had this wonderful experience growing up, so I decided to compile these 800 sayings.

"800 SAYINGS BY OLD FOLKS WHO RAISED US"

Compiled by Wm. Rocky Brown, 3rd

1. *I'm fixin' to*

2. *You reap what you sow*

3. *You can lead a horse to the water, but you can't make him drink. But you can salt his oats*

4. *Going down yonder*

5. *Sit down and behave*

6. *Ain't got enough sense to pour piss out of a boot with instructions on the bottom*

7. *Wrench me that...*

8. *What is hidden in the dark comes out in the light*

9. *One for the money Two for the show Three to get ready and Four to go*

10. *The pot talking about the kettle*

11. *The top calling the pot black*

12. *You ain't nothing until you're something*

13. *I used to walk to school uphill both ways in the winter with no shoes*

14. *Get up lazy bones*

15. *I got eyes in the back of my head*

16. *Rat now*

17. *Chidlinns'*

18. *Don't you suck your teeth or roll your eyes when I'm talking to you*

19. *Don't make me smack the piss outta you*

20. *Pee on the fire and call in the dogs this hunt is over*

21. Walked right by me and didn't say cat, dog, or nuthin'

22. Do me one mo' gin

23. I'll knock yo' fool head off

24. One thing for sure and two for certain

25. I will knock your block off

26. You can take it.... Or leave it

27. Bout to have a conniption

28. Young-ins

29. Dumb as a doorknob

30. I bought you into this world and I'll take you out

31. Happy as a pig eating slop

32. Great day in the morning

33. Wat us gonna do

34. Colored folks...

35. Wretch-around here and get my Bible...

36. Boy....pull up ya britches

37. You ain't no kin uh mine

38. That's her Lil red wagon...she can push it or pull it

39. I'm ma beat yo ass

40. Fair to Midlin

41. I Reckon

42. Come on in the room where Jesus is the Doctor and get my oil

43. If it was a snake it would of jumped up and bit you

44. All righty now

45. Too big for your britches

46. Come in here & get grandmamma the rollin pin

47. A hard head make a soft behind

48. Every tub must stand on its own bottom

49. Finnina go

50. He is Casket Sharp

51. Over yonder

52. Gan gech me a switch na

53. Please be seen and not heard

54. Southerners that moved North always referred to the South as DOWN HOME

55. Wretch this here glass out for me

56. Is pig meat greasy

57. Child that boy is sewing his oats

58. Every shut eye ain't sleep and every goodbye ain't gone

59. Can't see the forest for the trees

60. Get your behind out of the road

61. *Bless his heart*

62. *I declare*

63. *Lawdie, Lawdie, I reckon you right*

64. *If it don't come out in the wash, it'll sure come out in the rinse*

65. *Money don't grow on trees*

66. *Come on y'all*

67. *What goes around comes around*

68. *Don't dish it if you can't take it*

69. *They were like two peas in a pod*

70. *Slap the taste out yo mouth*

71. *It takes two to tango*

72. *This is gonna hurt me more than hurt you*

73. *My stars and garters*

74. *You look like the wreck of the Hesperus*

75. *Your ears are so dirty you could grow tatters in there*

76. *You'd lose your head if it wasn't attached*

77. *If your friend jumped off a bridge, would you*

78. *I wouldn't give you two cents for that*

79. *You made your bed, now lie in it*

80. *Liar, liar, pants on fire*

81. Starve a cold, feed a fever

82. Lawd have mercy

83. A watched pot never boils

84. Ain't that the truth

85. Blood is thicker than water

86. Cat got your tongue

87. Butter him up

88. You always hurt the one you love

89. Easy as falling off a log

90. Ain't nothing going on but the rent

91. I can't hear my yeers

92. Grab every rag and string

93. The Lord willing and the creek don't rise

94. Y'all don't believe fat meat is greasy

95. First and last time

96. Sooner or later

97. Kids in Africa are starving and you don't want to eat

98. There is a tag for every rag

99. Taint dat da truth

100. Negroes and flies I do despise the more I see negroes
     the better I like flies

101. You have to dot every "I" and cross every "T"

102. Snake bites you once its the snakes fault, snake bites you twice its your fault

103. Just because the car looks good doesn't mean the oil is clean

104. I'll slap you into the middle of next week

105. I'm as full as a tick

106. You don't think your sh*t stink

107. Haven't seen that sense Skippy was a puppy

108. We going to the store and make groceries

109. Go get me a pop

110. Shumoan here right now

111. *A top for every pot*

112. *Don't have a pot to piss in or a window to throw it out*

113. *Look at me when I'm talking to you*

114. *The apple down fall to far from the tree*

115. *Children are to be seen and not heard*

116. *Great Day in the morning*

117. *I'll slap the black off ya*

118. *Birds of a feather, flock together*

119. *Stop running your mouth*

120. *I don't care what other children do, you're my child*

121. *You are old enough for your wants not to hurt you*

122. *As long as you are living in my house, don't you ever...*

123. *As long as you are living in my house, eating my food, sucking up my heat, wearing my clothes...etc. You will follow my rules*

124. *Negroes in Hell want ice water*

125. *I can show you better than I can tell you*

126. *He's in a heap of trouble*

127. *Now you cooking with fish grease*

128. *Lies have short legs and they soon run out*

129. *Quiet as it's kept*

130. *Don't let the left hand know what right hand is doing*

131. *Tain't wise*

132. *Ain't no fool like an old fool*

133. *You got sum tee*

134. *Rat a way*

135. *She is smelling her pee*

136. *He is smelling himself*

137. *Boy I seen you before you seen yourself*

138. *Big Poppa*

139. *Big Momma*

140. *Mother-dear*

141. I'm looking at you with my good eye

142. If the cow can jump over the level, then I can look at the devil

143. Fresh as dish water

144. Ain't the size of the ship that makes you sick, it's the motion in the ocean

145. Watch out there now

146. He ain't got nuff sense to bella a buzzard

147. Lord help me before I kill this child

148. I'm still holding on

149. No matter how high a bird flies he has to come back down to the ground to eat.

150. Get off your rusty dusty and do what I told you to do

151. You better ask God to put a jet in your behind

152. Won't He do it

153. Don't you ever

154. Been there, done that, got the T-Shirt to prove it

155. There's nothing new underneath the sun

156. Don't let the door hit you, where the good Lord split you

157. You have to crawl before you walk.

158. Loose lips sink ships

159. Someone has to haul the ashes

160. The early bird catches the worm

161. When grown folks are talking stay in a child's place

162. Sharp as a tack

163. Clean as the board of health

164. No tickey no laundry

165. It's a dirty job but somebody got to do it

166. Romance without finance don't stand a chance

167. Who's your daddy, who you gonna love

168. Stupid is as stupid does

169. God takes care of babies, drunks and fools

170. Hush that fuss

171. *Much a blige*

172. *Right-yonder*

173. *Your eyes may shine, your teeth may grit but none of this will you git*

174. *It's nothing like getting what you think you want*

175. *That don't amount to a hill of beans.*

176. *When you see the saw dust flying you know the mill ain't far*

177. *Why buy the cow when you can get the milk for free*

178. *Every man got to ride his own mighty cloud of joy*

179. *You don't miss your water until the well runs dry*

180. *Get your ducks in a row*

181. Get your house in order

182. Momma's baby and daddy's maybe

183. Got to many cooks in the kitchen

184. Don't take no wooden nickels

185. They are just like crabs in a barrel

186. It ain't no fun when the rabbit got the gun

187. God works in mysterious ways

188. A dog that will bring a bone will sho-nuff carry a bone

189. Let it roll off your back like a duck in the rain

190. He can sell ice to Eskimos

191. *Cheaters never win*

192. *Don't nobody want a bone but a dog*

193. *They think Mr. Charlie's ice is colder*

194. *The Lord will make a way some how*

195. *Money is the root of all evil*

196. *Six in one hand half a dozen in the other*

197. *One mans trash is another mans treasure*

198. *A closed mouth doesn't get fed*

199. *Time flies when you're having fun*

200. *Fool me once shame on you fool me twice shame on me*

201. *If it looks like a duck and walks like a duck it must be a duck*

202. *You can put lipstick on a pig but its still a pig*

203. *Its my way or the highway*

204. *Still waters run deep*

205. *You play with fire you get burnt*

206. *Where there's smoke there's fire*

207. *You make your bed you got to lie in it*

208. *I pay the cost to be the boss*

209. *He who pays the piper names the tune*

210. *Don't make a mountain out of a molehill*

211. Its raining cats and dogs

212. You gotta know when to hold em and when to fold em

213. If the shoe fits wear it

214. Piss in my eye and tell me it's rain

215. Its a thin line between love and hated

216. Birds of a feather flock together

217. Let sleeping dogs lie

218. Don't throw the baby out with the bath water

219. It's your thing do what you wanna do

220. Jesus on the Mainline tell Him what you want

221. *She lies like a rug*

222. *Age ain't nuthin but a number*

223. *If it ain't broke don't fix it*

224. *It takes two to tango*

225. *Don't throw the rock then hide your hand*

226. *So glad I woke up clothed in my right mind*

227. *Sometimes you gotta get your hands dirty*

228. *You win some you lose some*

229. *Its not about winning its how you play the game*

230. *Time waits for no man*

231. *Trying to make a dollar out of 15 cents*

232. *A tiger never changes its strips*

233. *Beating a dead horse*

234. *Its cheaper to keep her*

235. *No love lost between them*

236. *All I want is a piece of the pie*

237. *What happens in this house stays in this house*

238. *Don't spill the beans*

239. *Don't cry over spilled milk*

240. *Blind as a bat*

241. *No news is good news*

242. *If you don't have nothing nice to say don't say nothing at all*

243. *I brought you in this world and I'll take you out*

244. *Back to the drawing board*

245. *Don't put your foot in your mouth*

246. *He beat her like he was beating a rattle snake*

247. *This is where the rubber meets the road*

248. *Where there's smoke there's fire*

249. *Sh*t or get off the pot*

250. *As long as I owe you you'll never be broke*

251. The apple don't fall far from the tree

252. He's a little piss ant

253. Red red pee in the bed lick it up with jelly and bread

254. Don't be stuck on stupid

255. The mind is a terrible thing to waste

256. If you like it I love it

257. You got to bring some ass to beat some ass

258. Mind your business

259. Sugar Honey Ice Tea

260. Kiss my grits

261. Your head is so pointy you think you are sharp

262. You all in the Kool-aid and don't know the flavor

263. Iron and steel will wear out so will flesh and bones

264. Don't hang with zeros

265. Bigger birds on higher limbs

266. A woman is like a bus you miss one another is coming in 15 minutes

267. Farrows know all medlows

268. Keep picking cotton and making plans

269. You too good til' you no good

270. Sometimes you got to cuss them out until they remember next time.

271. *If it ain't one thing it's another*

272. *If It ain't one thing it's two or three*

273. *You don't use your head for anything but hat rack*

274. *I can look through water and see dry land*

275. *Mean what you say and say what you mean*

276. *Still waters run deep*

277. *Your attitude is going to get you some assitude*

278. *At first you don't succeed try try again*

279. *Nothing beats a failure but a try*

280. *You gonna catch the death of pneumonia*

281. You need a hot toddy

282. If you don't know what to do with a little, you won't know what to do with a lot

283. Bless your heart

284. Shut yo mouth

285. They eat and sh*t like we do

286. It's twicks here and there

287. From huh to yunda

288. Empty the beer bottle

289. (HBO) Help a brother out

290. Sometimes you got to toot your own horn

291. Chew the meat and spit out the bones

292. You are so bright they should call you sunny

293. All is fair in love and war

294. Stay out of grown folks business

295. Put that in your pipe and smoke it

296. You can't have your cake and eat it too

297. Wrong as two left feet

298. Everything that shines ain't gold

299. He was butt naked

300. Howling at the moon

301. Too many fish in the sea

302. Pee you / P U

303. Don't hate the player hate the game

304. Good things come to those who wait

305. Don't judge me if you haven't walked a mile in my shoes

306. Believe half of what you see and none of what you hear

307. You break it you bought it

308. You have to know where you came from in order to know where you're going

309. A whistling woman and a crowing hen never comes to a very good end

310. Ain't that the berries

311. As easy as sliding off a greasy log backward

312. Barking up the wrong tree

313. Be like the old lady who fell out of the wagon

314. Busy as a stump-tailed cow in fly time

315. Caught with your pants down

316. Chugged full

317. Do go on

318. Don't bite off more than you can chew

319. Don't count your chickens before they hatch

320. Don't let the tail wag the dog

321. Don't let your mouth overload your tail

322. Either fish or cut bait

323. Even a blind hog finds an acorn now and then

324. Every dog should have a few feas

325. Fly off the handle

326. He got the short end of the stick

327. Give down the country

328. Go hog wild

329. Go off half-cocked

330. Go to bed with the chickens

331. *Go whole hog*

332. *Gone back on your raisin*

333. *Got your feathers ruffled*

334. *Happy as a dead pig in the sunshine*

335. *Have no axe to grind*

336. *Holler like a stuck pig*

337. *I do declare*

338. *In high cotton*

339. *In a coon's age*

340. *Like a bump on a log*

341. Mend fences

342. Scarce as hen's teeth

343. Sight for sore eyes

344. My old stomping grounds

345. Sun don't shine on the same dog's tail all the time

346. That takes the cake

347. Two shakes of a sheep's tail

348. Well, shut my mouth

349. Slow as molasses running uphill in the winter

350. Hold your horses

351. *Be back directly*

352. *Wait a cotton pickin' minute*

353. *Sit a spell*

354. *Take your own sweet time*

355. *Once in a blue moon*

356. *In a month of Sundays*

357. *Goin' to town*

358. *Goin' to hell in a hand basket*

359. *Precious*

360. *Yes M'am/Sir*

361. *Sug or Sugah*

362. *Cute as a button*

363. *Mind your P's & Q's*

364. *How's yer mama' n them*

365. *Say yer prayers/the blessin'*

366. *Oh suga foot*

367. *Suga britches*

368. *Heavens to Betsy*

369. *Suppa time*

370. *What in the Sam hill*

371. *I suwanne*

372. *What in tarnation*

373. *Well, I'll be*

374. *Up and at 'em*

375. *Y'all*

376. *All Y'all*

377. *Buggy*

378. *Gizzard*

379. *Clodhopper*

380. *Whatever suits your fancy*

381. *Happier than a dead pig in the sunshine*

382. *Wound tighter than a clock*

383. *Like white on rice*

384. *Proud as a peacock*

385. *Sick as a dawg*

386. *Don't hold water*

387. *Just like a bad refrigerator (Ice Box)*

388. *Knee high to a bullfrog / grasshopper / duck*

389. *Hotter than hell*

390. *The bigger they are the harder they fall*

391. *Playin' possum*

392. *Deader than a door nail*

393. *Plumb tuckered out*

394. *Tickled pink*

395. *Madder than a wet hen*

396. *Gettin' on my last nerve*

397. *Slap you silly*

398. *Me Myself and I*

399. *Fit to be tied*

400. *Don't get your feathers ruffled*

401. *The Lord will make a way somehow*

402. *Go outside and get me a switch*

403. *Gonna get a lickin'*

404. *Hush up*

405. *Fine and Dandy*

406. *Pinch a plug out of you*

407. *Quit yer bellyachin'*

408. *Quit bein' ugly*

409. *Flew off the handle*

410. *Cut that out*

411. *Raisin' cane*

412. *Like a bull in a china shop*

413. *Stinks to high heavens*

414. *You ain't right*

415. *Ragamuffin*

416. *High as a kite*

417. *Your face is gonna freeze like that*

418. *You weren't raised in a barn*

419. *Little Miss Prissy*

420. *Not the sharpest tool in the shed*

421. It's colder than a mother-in-law's love

422. Ding-dong

423. Lyin' like a dawg on a rug

424. Ain't just whistlin' Dixie

425. Slap yer mama

426. Sweatin' like a sinner in church

427. Hug yer neck

428. Gimme some sugar

429. Barkin' up the wrong tree

430. You can be in the slum but the slum don't have to be in you

431. *Your ears musta been burnin*

432. *Goodness gracious*

433. *Well I declare*

434. *You can't make a silk purse out of a sow's ear*

435. *Beatin' around the bush*

436. *Fine as frog's hair split four ways*

437. *Aggravating as a rock*

438. *She would argue with a fence post*

439. *Your mouth can block your blessings*

440. *Trouble don't last always*

441. *He's got a burr in his saddle*

442. *His knickers are in a knot*

443. *He can step in sh*t and come out smelling like a rose*

444. *She has a hissy fit with a tail on it*

445. *He has a duck fit*

446. *She has a dying duck fit*

447. *You're lower than a snake's belly in a wagon rut*

448. *He's slicker'n owl sh*t*

449. *She's meaner than a wet panther*

450. *He's a snake in the grass*

451. *Why, that egg-suckin' dawg*

452. *I been running all over hell's half acre*

453. *She's busier than a cat covering crap on a marble floor*

454. *I'm as busy as a one-legged cat in a sandbox*

455. *Busier than a moth in a mitten*

456. *She is about two sandwiches shy of a picnic*

457. *She ain't nothing but a gold digger*

458. *She's stuck up higher than a light-pole*

459. *She has her nose so high in the air she could drown in a rainstorm*

460. *He thinks the sun comes up just to hear him crow*

461. He squeezes a quarter so tight the eagle screams

462. He's tighter than a bull's ass at fly time

463. Tighter than a flea's ass over a rain barrel

464. He's so cheap he wouldn't give a nickel to see Jesus ridin' a bicycle

465. Too poor to paint, too proud to whitewash

466. I'm as poor as a church mouse

467. I'm so poor I can't afford to pay attention

468. He was so poor, he had a tumbleweed as a pet

469. I couldn't buy a hummingbird on a string for a nickel

470. I'm so poor I couldn't jump over a nickel to save a dime

471. *She is sharper than Mattie was when Dick died*

472. *Those pants were so tight I could see her religion*

473. *You're gonna have old and new-monia dressed like that*

474. *Lawd, people will be able to see Christmas*

475. *Lawd, pull that down We kin see clear to the promised land*

476. *It's so dry the trees are bribing the dogs*

477. *I swan, you all musta pissed God off somehow. It's drier than popcorn fart 'round these parts*

478. *He doesn't know whether to check his ass or scratch his watch*

479. *He couldn't find his ass with both hands in his back pockets*

480. *He's about as confused as a fart in a fan factory*

481. *She's lost as last year's Easter egg*

482. *These people don't know which way is up*

483. *He's as happy as if he had good sense.*

484. *Happier than ol' Blue layin' on the porch chewin' on a big ol' catfish head*

485. *You ain't nothing but a Jive Turkey*

486. *Grinnin' like a possum eatin' a sweet tater*

487. *Well that just dills my pickle*

488. *Won't hit a lick at a snake*

489. *He's about as useful as a steering wheel on a mule*

490. *Over-the-shoulder boulder holders*

491. *She gets my goose*

492. *He just makes my ass itch*

493. *Yankees are like hemorrhoids: Pain in the butt when they come down and always a relief when they go back up*

494. *That would make a bishop mad enough to kick in stained glass windows*

495. *She could make a preacher cuss*

496. *She could piss off the pope*

497. *If you don't stop that crying, I'll give you something to cry about*

498. *She could start an argument in an empty house*

499. *He is sharp as a tack*

500. *That makes about as much sense as tits on a bull*

501. *Quit goin' around your ass to get to your elbow.*

502. *Don't piss on my leg and tell me it's rainin'*

503. *Don't pee down my back and tell me it's raining*

504. *That dog won't hunt*

505. *You're lyin' like a no-legged dog*

506. *If his lips's movin', he's lyin'*

507. *You'd call an alligator a lizard*

508. *That man is talking with his tongue out of his shoe*

509. *He's as windy as a sack full of farts*

510. *Lying like a rug*

511. *If that boy had an idea, it would die of loneliness.*

512. *The porch light's on, but no one's home.*

513. *He's only got one oar in the water.*

514. *If brains were leather, he wouldn't have enough to saddle a junebug*

515. *He's so dumb, he could throw himself on the ground and miss*

516. *He hasn't got the sense God gave a goose*

517. *When the Lord was handin' out brains, that fool thought God said trains, and he passed 'cause he don't like to travel*

518. *His brain rattles around like a BB in a boxcar*

519. *There's a tree stump in a Louisiana swamp with a higher IQ*

520. *You got to have a "J-O-B" if you want to be with me*

521. He don't know sh*t from shinola

522. If his brains were dynamite, he couldn't blow his nose

523. Because there's snow on the roof doesn't mean that there's no fire in the furnace

524. Well butter my butt and call me a biscuit

525. Well, slap my head and call me silly

526. You little cotton-picker

527. He smelled bad enough to gag a maggot

528. Something smells bad enough to knock a dog off a gut wagon

529. I'm gonna cut your tail

530. I'm gonna jerk her bald

531. *Keep it up and I'll cancel your birth certificate*

532. *I am going to jerk a knot in your tail*

533. *You don't know dip sh** from apple butter*

534. *Me-n-you are gonna mix*

535. *You don't watch out, I'm gonna cream yo' corn*

536. *You better give your heart to Jesus, 'cause your butt is mine*

537. *I'll slap you to sleep, then slap you for sleeping*

538. *I'm gonna tan your hide*

539. *I'll knock you into the middle of next week looking both ways for Sunday*

540. *I'll knock you so hard you'll see tomorrow today*

541. *She's my sunshine on a cloudy day*

542. *Faster than a one-legged man in a butt-kicking competition.*

543. *Faster than green grass through a goose*

544. *Faster than a hot knife through butter*

545. *Slower than a Sunday afternoon*

546. *April showers bring May flowers*

547. *We're off like a herd of turtles*

548. *He ran like a scalded haint*

549. *It happened faster than a knife fight in a phone booth*

550. *He's so ugly, he didn't get hit with the ugly stick, he got whopped with the whole forest*

551. *He fell out of the ugly tree and hit every branch on the way down*

552. *She so ugly she'd make a freight train take a dirt road*

553. *He so ugly he'd scare a buzzard off a gut pile*

554. *She's so ugly I'd hire her to haunt a house*

555. *If I had a dog as ugly as you, I'd shave his butt and make him walk backwards*

556. *She is so ugly, her face would turn sweet milk to clabber*

557. *I feel like I've been chewed up and spit out*

558. *I feel like I been 'et by a wolf and sh*t over a cliff*

559. *He looks like ten miles of bad road*

560. *You look like you've been rode hard and put up wet*

561. *Fat as a tick*

562. *He's cooler than Cola on ice*

563. *He's so skinny, if he stood sideways and stuck out his tongue, he'd look like a zipper*

564. *She's so skinny, you can't even see her shadow*

565. *She's spread out like a cold supper*

566. *If he were an inch taller, he'd be round*

567. *Sh*ttin' in high cotton*

568. *He's richer'n Croesus*

569. *He's so rich he buys a new boat when he gets the other one wet*

570. *I'm so hungry my belly thinks my throat's been cut*

571. I'm so hungry I could eat the north end of a south-bound goat

572. Colder than a well digger's butt in January

573. It was colder than a witch's tit in a brass bra

574. That rain was a real frogwash

575. It rained like a cow pissin' on a flat rock

576. Hotter than blue blazes

577. It's colder than a penguin's balls

578. It's hotter than two rabbits screwin' in a wool sock

579. It's cold enough to freeze the balls off a pool table

580. Colder than a banker's heart on foreclosure day at the widows' and orphans' home

581. It's been hotter'n a goat's butt in a pepper patch

582. It's cold enough to freeze the tit off a frog

583. It is hotter than a jalapeño's coochie

584. There's more than one way to skin a cat

585. Bless your pea-pickin' little heart

586. Kiss my go-to-hell

587. I wouldn't walk across the street to piss on him if he was on fire

588. If you can't run with the big dogs, stay on the porch

589. Why so sad? Did Chevrolet stop makin' trucks

590. Deep in the South sushi is still called bait

591. He's about as useful as a screen door on a submarine

592. That sticks in your throat like a hair in a biscuit

593. You're so fulla sh*t your eyes are brown

594. He was as nervous as a long-tailed cat in a room full of rocking chairs

595. Wrong as two left shoes

596. The blacker the berry the sweeter the juice

597. Talk is cheap

598. Actions speak louder than words

599. Beauty is only skin deep and ugly is too the bone

600. You get what you give

601. *Nuthin' comes to a sleeper but a dream*

602. *You can't teach an old dog new tricks*

603. *Papa was a rolling stone wherever he laid his hat was his home*

604. *Put ya money where your mouth is*

605. *Girl you, preaching to the choir*

606. *I heard it through the grapevine*

607. *Keepin up with the Jones'*

608. *He's just like a rabbit jumping from hole to hole*

609. *If you lie...you steal...if you steal...you kill*

610. *Dont let your mouth write a check your ass can't cash*

611. He's crying wolf

612. Ain't nuthin' going on but the rent

613. Speak when spoken to

614. That suga daddy gonna rot her teeth

615. Monkey see monkey do

616. When you in Rome you do as the Romans do

617. I'll slap the taste out ya mouth

618. You gotta beat them to the punch

619. She wears her feelings on her sleeves

620. Tell the truth and shame the devil

621. You gotta climb the ladder to get to the roof

622. What goes around comes around

623. Talkin' loud and sayin' nuthin'

624. You may start it but imma' finish it

625. Keep your friends close and your enemies closer

626. If you live in a glass house you shouldn't throw stones

627. You can run but you can't hide

628. Pretty is as pretty does

629. Eat your food and let that shut your mouth

630. Don't use your fingers use your bread as your pusher

631. You ain't seen nothing yet

632. If a bullfrog had wings he wouldn't bump his ass when he jumped

633. Close that hole

634. Your ass is grass and I'm the lawnmower

635. Don't you make eyes at me boy

636. Opinions are like assholes some are just louder and smellier than others

637. Flatter than a gander's arch

638. That woman had forty 'leven kids

639. I had to go around my elbow to get to my thumb'

640. He's so clumsy he'd trip over a cordless phone

641. He's about as handy as a back pocket on a shirt

642. Shake what your momma gave ya

643. He couldn't carry a tune if he had a bucket with a lid on it

644. She was so tall she could hunt geese with a rake

645. She was so tall if she fell down she would be halfway home

646. He was so fat it was easier to go over top of him than around him

647. Poppa don't take no mess

648. No I'm not falling asleep I was just checking for holes in my eyelids

649. Bill's busier than a one-legged man at a butt kickin contest

650. Faster than a bell clapper in a goose's ass

651. *Gad night a livin'*

652. *Higher than a Georgia pine*

653. *I'm fixin' to go down the road a piece*

654. *Well, I'll just swaney*

655. *Don't go off with your pistol half cocked*

656. *We better git on the stick*

657. *Dumb as a bucket of rocks*

658. *She's got more nerve than Carter's got Liver Pills*

659. *He older than dirt*

660. *She's the knee-baby of the family*

661. *I feel like the last pea at pea-time*

662. *He wouldn't pay a dime to see a pissant pull a freight train*

663. *He'd have to stand up twice to cast a shadow*

664. *She'd complain if Jesus Christ came down and handed her a $5 bill*

665. *It's drier than happy hour at the Betty Ford clinic*

666. *I'm happier than a dog with two peters*

667. *I'll knock you in the head and tell God you died*

668. *She always looks like she stepped out of a band box*

669. *Act like you got some raising*

670. *You're the spitting image of your mother/father*

671. *Sunday go-to-meetin' clothes*

672. *Fish or cut bait*

673. *Egg-sucking dawg*

674. *I'm goin to the Juke joints*

675. *Drunker than Cooter Brown*

676. *Well he/she's just down rite sorry*

677. *Plumb fell off*

678. *You sure are poor*

679. *Well if that don't put pepper in the gumbo*

680. *He could tear up a railroad track with a rubber hammer*

681. *You must of spit that baby out*

682. *Well thank you Billy Sunday*

683. *If wishes were horses, then beggars would ride*

684. *Go cut me a switch*

685. *You better straighten up and fly right*

686. *I'll knock your teeth down your throat and you'll spit 'em out in single file*

687. *Knee high to a grasshopper*

688. *It's colder than Digger O'Dell, the friendly undertaker*

689. *Well ain't he just the tom-cat's kitten*

690. *I swalla'd down my Sun'de throat*

691. Wash down as far as Possible, wash up as far as Possible, then wash Possible

692. I swanky Mama shoulda named me Grace

693. Well he's got the same britches to get glad in

694. Get your butt off your shoulders

695. It's no skin off my nose if he wants to do that

696. God love 'im somebody's gotta

697. Too many chiefs and not enough Indians

698. If you lost something look where it ain't

699. What you do in the dark will come to the light

700. I'm on my way to see a dog about pig

701. A little bird told me

702. What's good for the goose is good for the gander

703. When I get on you I am going to pay you for old and new

704. The fruit don't fall to far from the tree

705. A hit dog will holla

706. She ain't nothing but an old nasty hoe

707. He's my sugar-daddy

708. He's got a big old Tombstone on top of a little dead body

709. You can't judge a book by its cover

710. The more you cry the less you piss

711. A penny saved is a penny earned

712. A rolling stone gathers no moss

713. All that glitters is not gold

714. An empty wagon makes a lot of noise

715. Tip for the day Look both ways before crossing the streets

716. A stitch in time saves nine

717. A wise man listens to his own conscience

718. Back seat driver

719. Be careful what you wish for you might get it

720. Be that as it may

721. *Better safe than sorry*

722. *Beware of burning your bridges when you cross them*

723. *Black sheep of the family*

724. *Blind in one eye and can't see out of the other*

725. *Blood is thicker than water*

726. *Break a mirror and you will have seven years bad luck*

727. *Burning the candle at both ends*

728. *Burning the midnight oil*

729. *Calm before the storm*

730. *Can't live with them and can't live without them*

731. Can't see the forest for the trees

732. Catch some Z's

733. Caught between a rock and a hard place

734. Clothes don't make the man

735. Cloud nine

736. Coast is clear

737. Cold as ice

738. Cold hands - warm heart

739. Cold shoulder

740. Cold turkey

741. Come hell or high water

742. Cooked his goose

743. Ya'll gonna make me loose my mind and hurt somebody

744. Couldn't hit the broad side of the barn

745. Count your blessings, not your problems

746. Day late and a dollar short

747. Dead as a doornail

748. Dead men tells no tales

749. Dig your own grave

750. Do as I say do and not as I do

751. Do or die

752. Doesn't have a leg to stand on

753. Doesn't have two nickels to rub together

754. Don't bite off more that you can chew

755. Don't bite the hand that feeds you

756. You bout to speak out

757. Don't beat a dead dog

758. Your eyes are bigger than your stomach

759. Don't beat around the bush

760. Double dog dare

761. Easy come easy go

762. Eat crow

763. Eat drink and be merry

764. Eat your heart out

765. Eaten out of house and home

766. Enough is enough

767. Experience is the best teacher

768. Fair weather friend

769. Few and far between

770. Fit to be tied

771. Fits him to a T

772. Go for broke

773. Go off half cocked

774. Go with the flow

775. God helps those who help themselves

776. God moves in mysterious ways

777. God bless the child who has his own

778. Going to be a cold day in hell

779. Goodie two shoes

780. Got my mojo working

781. I can't make head or tails of it

782. If you are not part of the solution, you are part of the problem

783. If you can't beat them join them

784. Shake rattle and roll

785. Time to cut a rug

786. If you can't say anything nice don't say anything

787. If you can't stand the heat, get out of the kitchen

788. Just hunkey dory

789. Knock on wood

790. Lesser of two evils

791. It ain't over til the fat lady sings

792. God don't like ugly

793. That's funny as a three-legged dog in a horse race

794. Give him two nickels for a dime and he'll think he's rich

795. I'm busier than a 2-dollar whore on nickel night

796. She can start an argument in an empty house

797. The porch light is on but no one is home

798. Running like a chicken with it's head cut off

799. He's one fry short of a Happy Meal

800. If everything is coming your way you're in the wrong lane